"Bizarre. Brutal. Honest. Strangely relatable. . . . There are no weak poems in *Now We're Getting Somewhere*, but the segment titled Confessional Poetry could easily be called its crowning jewel." —Gabino Iglesias, *PANK*

"Kim Addonizio tells you outrageous truths about the world and the human heart. . . . Addonizio's poems trust us to hear bad news, as they puncture one sentimentality after another in a way that's wildly pleasurable and addictive. . . . Through her wit, inventive absurdities, delicious range of tones (defiant, savoring, stricken), and surprising poetic forms, Addonizio turns into poetry the shameful, contradictory, messy parts of ourselves we normally keep most tucked away." —Adam Scheffler, *Harvard Review*

"Several moments in these poems suggest a universal despair and loneliness that feels in keeping with the present moment, but Addonizio's incredible comedic timing and brilliance at subverting the reader's expectations ensures the mood is never too dark for long. These poems are brilliant reflections from the high priestess of the confessional." —*Publishers Weekly*, starred review

"It's true that this collection is shot through with 'confessional poetry,' which, in the wrong hands can make for some dreadful navel-gazing, but Addonizio's unfailing bullshit detector is always first pointed at herself, and her work is so just damned much fun to read that it's easy to see why she is one of America's most popular poets." —David Starkey, *California Review of Books*

"[Addonizio] explores how the confessional is a genre to work within by tying risqué sex to high-minded intellectual theory to the self-indulgence of social media in a single brushstroke that brilliantly critiques the label of 'confessional poet.' . . . To follow Addonizio is be enlivened by the daring personal revelation of a confession while also experiencing her poetry on a stage of ideas." —Grant Faulkner, *Rumpus*

"Another knockout collection. . . . [I]n Addonizio's treatment, subjects as various as misogyny, climate change, hotel bars, literary critics, convalescence, orgasms and John Keats become heartbreaking, gut-busting, shattering." —*Shelf Awareness*

"Gutsy poems that are also funny and accessible. . . . [Addonizio] invokes many of her influences by name in *Now We're Getting Somewhere*: Plath, Sexton, Colette, Woolf, maybe especially Dorothy Parker, with whom [she] shares a cynical, sarcastic, dark humor." —John Yohe, *Splice Today*

"Addonizio delivers enough electricity to light up any room—or light up a reader's imagination, raging mind, gentle and/or isolated and suffering heart." —Lou Fancher, *48hills*

NOW WE'RE GETTING SOMEWHERE

POEMS

KIM ADDONIZIO

W. W. NORTON & COMPANY
Independent Publishers Since 1923

For information about permission to reproduce selections from this book, write to
Permissions, W. W. Norton & Company, Inc., 500 Fifth Avenue, New York, NY 10110

For information about special discounts for bulk purchases, please contact
W. W. Norton Special Sales at specialsales@wwnorton.com or 800-233-4830

Manufacturing by LSC Harrisonburg
Production manager: Beth Steidle

Library of Congress Cataloging-in-Publication Data

Names: Addonizio, Kim, 1954– author.
Title: Now we're getting somewhere : poems / Kim Addonizio.
Other titles: Now we are getting somewhere
Description: First Edition. | New York, NY : W. W. Norton & Company, [2021]
Identifiers: LCCN 2020051547 | ISBN 9780393540895 (hardcover) |
ISBN 9780393540901 (epub)
Subjects: LCGFT: Poetry.
Classification: LCC PS3551.D3997 N69 2021 | DDC 811/.54—dc23
LC record available at https://lccn.loc.gov/2020051547

ISBN 978-1-324-02194-0 pbk.

W. W. Norton & Company, Inc., 500 Fifth Avenue, New York, N.Y. 10110
www.wwnorton.com

W. W. Norton & Company Ltd., 15 Carlisle Street, London W1D 3BS

1 2 3 4 5 6 7 8 9 0

FOR THE MAKERS

Everybody knows the captain lied.

—LEONARD COHEN

Pour yourself a drink, put on some lipstick, and pull yourself together.

—ELIZABETH TAYLOR

CONTENTS

III. CONFESSIONAL POETRY   41

IV. ARCHIVE OF RECENT UNCOMFORTABLE EMOTIONS

I

NIGHT IN
THE CASTLE

NIGHT IN THE CASTLE

I'm not sure what to do about that scorpion twitching on the wall
Maybe I should slam it with this book of terrible poetry

or just read aloud to it until it dies of a histrionic metaphor
bleeding out on the ancient stones in a five-octave aria

If I get a little drunker I might try to murder it with my sandal
I gave up on mercy a while ago

That's what happens when you live in a castle on an artist's grant
You look at the late-afternoon Umbrian light smearing itself over the
    tomato vines

& feel entitled—like an underage duchess whose husband has finally died
    of gout
leaving her free for more secret liaisons with the court musician

She might even have poisoned the duke, the lecherous shit
It's hard to remember what life was like before this

& I don't want to, I want to stay here & poison the king next
I want to be a feared & beloved queen ordering up fresh linens &
    beheadings

locking up bad poets in their artisanal hair shirts
torturing academics with pornographic marionette performances

Meanwhile the scorpion is still there twitching slightly
reciting something about violence & the prison of ego

& I can hear the clashing armies on the wide lawn outside
sinking down into history & then standing up again

BLACK HOUR BLUES

Nothing is the new black's shit soundtrack.
The elk's black blood leaks from the roof rack.
Black the prospects of the destitute sick.

Blackberries suppurate in the pie tin.
Green cards burnt black in the gas-lit oven.
Black mold loitering in the privacy of prison.

Black Deepwater Horizon pelican and dolphin.
Through Standing Rock a black worm crawls.
Black Baltimore Mali Iraq Sudan Cambodia Sinai Selma *Uh*.

The darkling beetle raises its black back and runs
through the black Ghost Ship and Grenfell Tower ruins.
Black Syria Somalia Ferguson *Uh* Attica Gaza Yemen *Huh*.

Black heart weighed against an ostrich plume.
Blindfolded goddess, long sword drawn
nowhere in the *Oh* come down come down.

FIXED AND IN FLUX

The cicadas swarm the pines all summer,
the males flexing their tymbals to make
the horrifying sound that will attract a mate.
The new people are fidgeting in strollers,
running on little piston legs
hard toward the street, toward the breast
and then the beer can, and soon
the breast again. When one door closes,
another floats downriver
under the night sky. Nine planets
seemingly forever and then suddenly
Pluto's demoted. *The king is dead!*
Long live the king! Existentially,
we're either crawling toward
a top-shelf margarita being perfected by
adorable six-winged angels, or else
getting puréed in a food processor
on a decapitated mountain.
Meanwhile, a sea worm slithers through a mortgage.
72% of Americans believe in angels,
no wonder that parasitic amoeba got elected.
Meanwhile, a lake comes to realize
it's now a grenade.

ANIMALS

I think I could turn and live with animals

—WALT WHITMAN

O Walt you were wrong, they aren't placid or self-contained
I just watched a spoonbill make carpaccio out of a frog
& crocodiles dining on wildebeests trying to cross the Maro River

It's wrong to say *O* in poetry these days
which makes me want to have a loud orgasm right here
in an unashamed animal way

You must have been looking at some cows on a farm but who wants to live
    like that
standing around in a shed with sore tits, shitting claustrophobically
or standing around shitting & being tortured by flies & eating grass

I know you like grass but it's no fun to be a pricey pre-hamburger,
    ruminating with no TV
If you'd had a cable subscription maybe you would have felt differently
watching *NatGeo Wild* & those exhausted herds on the Serengeti

Walt, I still love you even if in this instance you might have been a victim
    of the pastoral tradition
Let me tell you about animals: The green anaconda swallowed the young
    capybara whole

O o oh oh oh *OHHHH* Walt
Capybaras are the largest rodents on earth

I don't think I'd survive as an animal for long, even a large one—Look at
    the elephants
Imagine being murdered & becoming a doodad
or furniture inlay

Walt, I actually like sweating & whining about my condition
Hot flashing & bitching in my cream satin sheets, lying awake drunk &
    weeping in the dark
I'd definitely like to own more things

An electric knife sharpener for instance would come in handy
for carving up the less fortunate on special holidays
I want to be lucky as long as I can

Walt, Walt, I don't think death is luckier or leads life forward like you said
I don't think I'm going to grow from the grass you love
I'm just going to have one last blackout in a dirty pink lace dress
& be eaten by tiny ugly legless larvae

COMFORT OF THE RESURRECTION

One day everything that's over or dead

will come back, oil painting & God,

chivalry & the kings (even the mad

old rotters, why not, while the heads

of the plotters are removed

from their iron spikes & carefully glued

on again)—why not believe in the miracle—plaid

has already come back so why not the starved

& flooded corpses, why not fresh bread

from charred toast, aren't the grubbers in the cupboard

constantly churning up from the charnel the old

ingredients, holy seed, holy blood,

nothing is ever destroyed,

but tell that to Marianna whose child

lived for three days brainless & blind

close by cheap factories on the filthy Rio Grande,

tell it to all the ruined & annulled

residents of the earth, everything

& everyone will be restored

& immortal diamonds will soon be yours.

GRACE

Let go & let God is my guard dog Beware
the ragged shithole hordes & bless
my chrome moly Bushmaster .223 rest

your asses nowhere near my rod & staff
I raise my beacon-hand &
torch anyone who doesn't believe Jesus

was calved from a virgin & then ascended
to his penthouse & will raptor down
to smite Jews abortionists niggers

Muslims fags Obama the AntiChrist SATAN
WAS THE FIRST TO DEMAND EQUAL RIGHTS
outside the Knoxville Baptist Tabernacle

while a boy puts his tongue in another boy's mouth
& they lie down together shy & barely breathing

HIGH DESERT, NEW MEXICO

Temple of the rattlesnake's religion.
Deluge and heat-surge. Crèche of the atom's
rupture. Night blackens like a violin
and bright flour falls from the kitchens of heaven.
This is where the seams begin to loosen,
where you can walk for miles in any direction—
rabbit, lizard, raven, insect drone—
and almost forget the shame of being human.
Smoke tree. Sage. Not everything is broken.
Horses appear at this remote cabin
to stand outside and wait for you to come
with a single apple. Abandon
your despair, you who enter here forsaken.
The wind is saying something. Listen.

SIGNS

This morning the East River Ferry is just a boat pulling up to the ugly little
  park in Williamsburg
& Manhattan isn't the underworld projecting its eternal office buildings
  into those clouds
The seagull landing on my balcony isn't an image of transcendence or
  being destroyed by love

There isn't any meaning in things
There probably aren't even any things
which is hard to think about & this morning I don't want to think about
  anything

but I do, I think about . . . things
as each special, unique individual in the long line below my window steps
  onto the ferry
as rain slips down not representing the Many cleaved from the One & black
  umbrellas unfold

I think about the giant wax man in the museum with three wicks in his
  head slowly burning
& the hollow as his face starts to melt from the inside
& the heartsick woman who jumped from the bridge, hauled up & covered
  with a tarp on the dock

I'm sick of death & sick to death of romantic love but I still want to live
if only to rearrange the base metals of my depression
like canned lima beans on a mid-century modern dinner plate

My last love had beautiful green eyes
Eyes like two caged parrots refusing to say anything
Eyes like two rivers filling with toxic runoff

Maybe later today the sun will come out & smile like a kind nanny
but it won't be a kind nanny, or even a mean nanny, shaking me hard
One day it will just cool, like . . . a star

When the clock says 11:11 it doesn't mean
the design of things has risen to the surface & been made manifest
It means I'm still here hours later watching the boats dock & then leave
    without me

It means the people who commuted across the river to work on Wall Street
are still there, their eyes like suitcases of small, unmarked bills
& everything is going to change for the worse

THE EARTH IS ABOUT USED UP

like a sodden tampon & no place to throw it away

like an armpit-yellowed vintage blouse with see-through pearl bubble sleeves

like a tissue travel pack in a foreign bathroom & you have to squat over a
    hole in the floor

The earth is about used up, is the point I'm trying to drunkenly steer
    through the potholed streets

into the suburban garage of your ears

though you probably already know what's up with the earth, but I am
    telling you because

because because because because because

The earth is about used up

like the preserved atrophied brain of a retired NFL defensive lineman
    leaking cryoprotectant

like the tender ass of the cow & the large heart of the racehorse

like a wind-up ladybug, ladybug

crawling in decelerating circles on LuxTouch marble tiles inlaid with
    precious stones

Even the ocean is gasping for air

while someone smokes a cigarette through their throat-hole

& sodas go flat in the heat

& a stack of *National Geographic*s bloats in a rained-on cardboard box in a
    fallen shed

some animal dragged itself into to shit away its life

I'm standing on that box with my teeny megaphone, bringing you the news
    you know

wildly virtue signaling waving my mortal handkerchief dropping it at your
    feet

where it burns it burns here I don't want it you take it please you take it

IN BED

The world is like an ugly person you're supposed to love for their inner
    beauty
but some people are just ugly—if you poke them with a short needle
you find badly lit rooms of cheap wall-to-wall carpet
& metal shelves of racially insensitive trinkets
so it's often better to avoid them completely
& mind your own business . . . in bed

Today is a good day to get things done . . . in bed
An atmospheric river has closed the zoo, the elephants are trudging
    through the mud
Trees are falling over like myotonic goats & not getting up again
At the bottom of the river you're in a cozy submarine . . .

Cats asleep on either side of you . . .
as you think about Colette, who spent her last years in her apartment in the
    Palais-Royal . . .
with her phone & books & papers
Time wrote that her novels were about "quietly desperate women in love &
    in bed"
but that's all the women I know except for the ones
whose beds are shallow graves

Sometimes it's fun when in love to grow loudly desperate . . .
and write about it . . .
especially when your lover has left you alone . . .
to be cradled by your Microbead Boyfriend Pillow in its striking azure T-shirt

There are so many things you can accomplish, at home . . .
You can meet all sorts of lovely people . . .
You can fake an orgasm to hurry things along . . .
because you would rather be out having brunch with bottomless mimosas
or binge-watching other people having sex

With a man or just some sperm & the right equipment you can get a baby
& then bring it in bed to sleep with you
until it grows up and leaves you alone . . .

But beds are not just for sex or procreation
or sleep, or sleeplessness smoldering with 4 a.m. dread
Beds are for living! Beds are for life . . .
& for memory, as you lie between cork-lined walls
writing very long sentences in French

Sometimes I'm so happy

I want to kill myself first thing in the morning to make sure I die . . .

under my white organic ruched duvet cover

like a marmot burrowed deep under the snow

who can't wake up from hibernation

while others crawl out, ravenous for spring

II

SONGS FOR
SAD GIRLS

WOLF SONG

At the party they're all wearing swan suits.
The fur on your back thickens. You're slicked
against the wall of the flow-through kitchen
between your ex and his girlfriend.
You'd still like to devour him as you once did,
but you are trying to become human.
Though also you are starving,
sick of scavenging nuts and berries,
gnawing the occasional biscuit.
You want to take down a caribou!
You want to tackle a moose and rip open
the flap of skin swaying beneath its throat
and share it with the next wolf
to trot by. But here there are no wolves.
Through the kitchen window fangs the moon
to fuck you up even more, to send you slathering
away, past the condo community,
past the lit houses, into the deep woods;
where there's a moon,
there's always a deep woods.

SONG FOR SAD GIRLS

Right now I feel like a self-cleaning microwave about to malfunction.
My friend texts from the east coast, *I smoked so many cigarettes in this chair.*

She's in some bar. Do people still even say, *old haunts*? She's sitting there
    with a second beer,
haunted by a sad girl. Now I feel more like a burn hole in a cushion,
still smoldering. A set of plastic curtains. *Whoosh,* I could go up any minute.

Sad girls, sad girls, you're everywhere. Sick on the snake oil
of romance. Blundering in and out of beds
and squabbles with roommates. Scalded by raindrops.
Hating yourselves with such a pure hatred.
Loving the music that makes it worse. This is that music.

There's a low piano part in here somewhere, sinking under a wave
of minor thirds. There's a plastic guitar with shitty strings and you think
you're that guitar nobody wants even for a weird art project. You don't know

that your trash and dead birds can cast beautiful shadows. You don't know
anything and I love you for that.

Right now I feel like a menthol filter. I float face-up in the toilet,

my lipstick dissolving, as crowds of girls swirl by. I creak like a rusted-out

   insect

trying to fly. I spin around and around

for you and you only, scraping out this old, sad song.

RÉSUMÉ

—*after Dorothy Parker*

Families shame you;

Rehab's a scam;

Lovers drain you

And don't give a damn.

Friends are distracted;

Aging stinks;

You'll soon be subtracted;

You might as well drink.

TELEPATHY

I don't know if telepathy has ever been proved or disproved
but when I go out with a friend & there's a man by himself . . . I feel . . . him . . .

Something goes out from me, little threads of energy, my invisible feelers begin
    waving,
my third eye on its stalk turns slowly . . . & if I've entered the circle of his
    awareness

where his pancakes are shrinking from his bacon . . . or his beer is wetting itself . . .
what messages are drifting into his hair . . . like cat dander . . .

like oversharing fortunes from insecure fortune cookies . . .
I am not a strong, independent person experiencing life to the full . . .

I never learn from my mistakes . . . Maybe you could be one of them . . .
Men like to say they're not mind readers, but the ones I'm drawn to aren't
    readers at all . . .

Their thought-balloons are full of dick pics . . . floating toward the ceiling
& slowly deflating, like their interest in me . . . Maybe telepathy is bunk, but
    magic sure isn't . . .

I remember a man who liked to dress me up . . . then saw me in half
& I stood up smiling & bowing . . .

SMALL TALK

Let's skip it and get straight to the rabid dog at hand.
This is some weather we're cowering from.
Would you please touch my face like a blind person?
I feel like a giraffe in a parking garage.
Let's skip it and get straight to the death smell
coming from behind the refrigerator.

Can I offer you something more subtly evocative
of the underlying theme of your life story?
How many self-important wounds do you have?
Everything you say is tiresome.
I'm going to walk away slowly and not look back.
Now we're getting somewhere.

GHOSTED

I guess you realized how worthless I am
I myself am just beginning to discover it . . .
Nothing is being named after me

A planet would be nice . . . or a star system
But I don't want to be anyone's sunbeam
Maybe a black hole . . . I just saw a picture of one

& oddly you weren't in it . . .
I don't care what you're wearing right now
as you don't think of me at all . . . I've already disappeared

like a dead girl in a police procedural
but you're not the detective . . . & I'm not dead . . .
Darling, there are plenty of nameless alleys

& I intend to walk down one late at night
howling at the trash bins until a light blinks on
& someone sets out a nice dish of gin . . .

AUGUST

What I want is to slice open its stomach and watch

its toxic sun uncoil into the sea.

Cicadas seething in their asylum in the trees.

All this frenzy and scorch

and at night music hammering from the outdoor bar

where the dancers blindside each other

with longing, and the long tide slopping

in and away, barnacles on the piers clinging

in the littoral drift. Whatever it is in me

that crawls like a wasp over the remains

of a picnic, used napkins blown

over the senseless grass—tell me

how to kill it. How to let it go out like the last

disaster of love, last boat guttering in the wave-swell.

WINTER SOLSTICE

I can't think about the black slick on the river or the deer

corpse at the base of the tree or how one lover is

too young & sometimes indifferent & another is

lighting candles with someone else neither

ever mine for more than a rare evening the days will

lengthen now but so slowly it will still

feel like darkness is winning the battle between

it & what people call good or God a few fallen trees

are always there in the woods turning back

to earth rump torn open a kind of caul

over the eyes maybe a coyote thick

film on the river a lover's hair lit fallen

trees lengthen now but so slowly I can't think

indifferent base God between either darkness

ALL HALLOWS

It's bad to be alone on Halloween, worse than spending Thanksgiving with
    a Styrofoam cup of Turkey Noodle
or a sober Christmas after a breakup, surrounded by happy lesbian couples
    discussing condo timeshares

You have to turn off your lights & hide from the doorbell
You have to cover your eyes from knife shadows on the walls
& your ears from sinister music scores, smashing window glass, & terrified
    girls

You have to remember that time as a kid you vomited all over your fairy
    outfit at the shopping center
& then peed out of shame, with your ripening talent for making things worse
You had a talent for singing, too—twice you lost competitions to boys
    playing the drum solo from "Wipeout"
You should have just stood up in the auditorium & done your retromingent
    trick in front of the entire school

Now you do it in poems, laying a golden sheen over the paper, inviting
    people in
to the dirty gas station bathroom of your performative loneliness
Princess, French maid, ladybug, cowgirl, zombie

It's the Night of the Living Ex-Husbands

The souls are pouring out of Purgatory or steaming up from the animals
    they were trapped in

My father wants a fresh beer, my mother some Fritos with a single
    bourbon-and-Coke

My brother just wants to go fishing one more time

Cheerleader, angel, skeleton, witch, imago

Round about the toilet go

In the fatal kisses throw

Oh my weird sisters, we're not bad, just lost—look at Anne Sexton swirling
    overhead

behind Plath & her impeccable broom, look at all the blottophiliac girls

longing to faceplant in Mr. Death's crotch

Ladies, women, darlings, bitches, you

Stop it right now & pay attention: Virginia Woolf is rising

from the river, sloshing home to Leonard in her Wellingtons

nothing in her pockets but bread

You have to take out the stones & put them back where they belong

You have to carve the names of the dead & then let rain & years destroy them

The moon weakening like a cheap flashlight while your heart blinks on

ALIENMATCH.COM

I am trying to center my spacecraft
over a volcano. I am six trillion years old
but am often mistaken for an asteroid.
My body type is indeterminate.
Sometimes I resemble a white marble floor
on which stained glass light diffusedly falls,
at other times an aortic clot.
The first thing people notice about me
is the caul over my third eye.
I would like to engage in heated conversation
about which is the dish sponge
and which the counter sponge.
I would like to date you
if you would acknowledge my special qualities
without my having to exhibit any.
After six trillion years, my spacecraft
is a little tired. Sometimes I spend
whole nights trying to phone
my dead parents, running from tigers,
looking for a condom. Mostly I feel
confused as a daffodil who didn't get
the memo about fluttering. I keep trying
to wake up in my dreams. If I didn't
know better, I might think you were in them.

TO THE WOMAN CRYING UNCONTROLLABLY IN THE NEXT STALL

If you ever woke in your dress at 4 a.m. ever
closed your legs to someone you loved opened
them for someone you didn't moved against
a pillow in the dark stood miserably on a beach
seaweed clinging to your ankles paid
good money for a bad haircut backed away
from a mirror that wanted to kill you bled
into the back seat for lack of a tampon
if you swam across a river under rain sang
using a dildo for a microphone stayed up
to watch the moon eat the sun entire
ripped out the stitches in your heart
because why not if you think nothing &
no one can / listen I love you joy is coming

WAYS OF BEING LONELY

Like a haunted river no bridge wants to lay itself down over.

Like a taxidermied grizzly in the Student Union.

You cry at a frequency only subatomic insects can hear.

That time with him in Houston.

Sometimes you flame into a scary flower.

An eruption of coherence in the post-modern seminar.

You stand in a shallow creek & your reflection floats slowly downstream
without you.

Alcohol is your emotional support animal.

The fan hums erratically.

An unclaimed suitcase of miniature toiletries, burst open on the baggage
carousel.

Like an amoeba without an e-scooter.

An extra in an epic battle scene, trampled by a non-equity horse.

You're a red-breasted flute, but everyone else is a dowel.

A Zen koan blooming in the White House Rose Garden.

Sun-damaged curtains in the parlor of an abandoned friendship.

You're the queen, but you're a bee being sucked into the pool's filtration
    system.

Like a version, touched for the very last time.

Spooky piano music rising from the dishwater.

You wake up alone to a bird reciting Keats.

GUITAR

Sometimes it sleeps in its case all day like a stringed vampire
In the store down the street its friends are hanging like hams
Guitars, like hearts, can be anything

If you really want to break your lover's heart it's simple
Just immerse yours in tepid water & walk out of the kitchen
Go call someone you always wanted & play them a song on your new guitar

Don't break your own guitar unless you happen to be a guitar god
in which case go ahead & smash it with the impunity befitting a god
Also feel free to smash your chosen people while reminding them how
    much you love them

My guitar is often depressed because it takes itself seriously
as the instrument of a few generations of sensitive singer-songwriters
The ukulele has lately grown in popularity but a uke is so babyish
Playing it is like trying to placate a god by ritual murdering a sacrificial
    blankie

When my guitar is sad it glows eloquently & goes berserk
thinking of light thinning in a hospital gown
& the sound of paper slippers on gray linoleum
like a voice being mopped off the tiles

A guitar, like a heart, has a hole in it

It heaves out its music like a twerking volcano

like a faucet leaking bluebells in a gutted house

Heart like the last Red Wolf

in the decimated population of eastern North Carolina

looking for a mate

Heart like a target

Hole like an exit wound

Play on

III

CONFESSIONAL POETRY

Writing it is like firing a nail gun into the center of a vanity mirror

or slowly shaking a souvenir snow-globe of asbestos & shame

to quiet an imaginary baby

It's like sewing rhinestones on your traumas so you can wear them to a
    pain festival

or beating a piñata selfie with a pink rubber bat
so you can pet the demons that fall out

No, the confessional is a mode among other modes

Right now I'm getting fingered in a museum bathroom during a Cindy
    Sherman exhibit
while discussing Susan Sontag's "The Pornographic Imagination"

& live streaming it on Instagram
Why don't you follow me

A beef-witted male critic is indexing my sins

in a highly regarded literary publication

Supergluing my clitoris forever to the pillar of historical irrelevance

It's shitting your fancy gown in a home movie & everyone who loves you
     recoiling
while you shrug because it's only a movie

Doing a clever impersonation of roadkill in glitter eyeshadow
then lifting up your dress to show everyone your invisible dirty panties

Not wearing waterproof mascara while you're being tasered

Staging your copycat suicide, leaving lipstick on your noose

You open a vein of hematite & convince everyone it's blood

then bleed out on a white shag carpet

All over the world, depressed, narcissistic little bitches
are filling notebooks with their feelings

Sloppy, boring, grotesque, unfuckable feelings

I really like feeling something when I stagger into a poem

& having a place to lie down & cry

I woke up this morning from uneasy dreams & put on three pairs of tiny
   high heels
Embed me in plastic, pass me around

Put me onstage so I can stand over a grave trap
& a man can explain what's wrong with me

Rape me by the light of the moon shining over a nuclear reactor pool

Is there a single idea in my pretty little head?

Let's have another cocktail & find out
while I remove these sticky bandages

IV

ARCHIVE OF
RECENT
UNCOMFORTABLE
EMOTIONS

PEOPLE YOU DON'T KNOW

You have no idea what's inside them.
Slipped gears and downed wires, rotted-out floor planks.
Maybe anemones.
Maybe a billion spiral galaxies.

There's the famously beautiful famous poet you once saw through an open
    bathroom door
projectile vomiting into a sink before the door swung closed again.

You're afraid to open that boxed case of wine, certain a mouse got trapped
    inside
but it's only Styrofoam rubbing against more Styrofoam
like the sex you used to have with people you didn't know.

Some people smile when they hate you.
Wracking sobs are usually a good indication
they've been gutted by fire.
Liars are supposed to be betrayed by the direction their eyes dart
but good liars know this, so the truth is anyone's guess.

Eye contact may be indicative of rudeness
or the early delusional phase of love.
The early delusional phase of love.
The early delusional phase of love.

When a woman at a party says, *I like your necklace*
a multiverse of possible interpretations yawns open like a meat-eating plant.

Sometimes it's better to stay in the lobby, where the bar is,
so as not to discover the creeping mold in a room with a parking lot view.
Then again, if that stranger absorbing vodka a few stools down
would only glance your way, and give you a sign,
you just might go there.

EX

When I think about him now I think about the money he stole from me
I remember the mice in his couch & the dying fish in his aquarium
& also feeling like a gilded royal barge was ceremoniously moving through
   my blood

while LED snow fell theatrically in the folds of my brain
I remember thinking nothing could ruin our love which is what everyone
   thinks at first
but it turns out everyone is wrong

Some things are destined to be ruined
Cheap dresses student housing self-esteem romantic projections
Ice sculptures of dead jazz musicians turning to mush in the rain

Some of the fish did themselves in, leaping out past the filter & over the edge
Others just flipped over & floated up & started looking kind of shredded
Mostly I think about how little I think about him now

like he was just some decorative saltwater display in an overpriced lobby
or a hangover I sweated out in a single low-impact cardio-weight routine
when once he was the creature who swallowed me whole

in a huge religiously significant way

THE TRUTH

You could spend all day bored and unhinged,
counting to a thousand, closing the windows,
terrified by leaves. Look at your hand, it won't
open to reveal what's coming. Nothing
changes but everything has already and that's what
you hate, prodded forward with a stick, stumbling
after some elusive, half-imagined creature.
Studying its entrails. Bending over its scat.
When all the time it's stalking you. When
all the time it's got you by the throat.
Below your window, some little kids are walking in
single file, roped together, through the intersection.
Their teacher—or minder—yanks them along.
You watch them without any feeling. Or with one that's wrong.

ARCHIVE OF RECENT UNCOMFORTABLE EMOTIONS

The this haircut makes me feel ugly feeling

The however much I drink I can't pretend it's love feeling

The strangled by the foul and ugly mists of vapours in iambic pentameter
feeling

The everything I write is shit feeling

The I'm sorry I gave you those blow jobs and did you not understand the
meaning of "reciprocal" feeling

The it's not my birthday anymore I'm just older feeling

The looking at X-rays of my teeth feeling

The something died in your eyes and I can smell it feeling

The literary recognition might be just another shiny object feeling

The darkling I listen and right now I think it would be kind of cool to die
feeling

The Keats is dead feeling

The Leonard Cohen is dead feeling

The _____ and _____ and my _____ are also quite dead feeling

The I am Jean Rhys getting blotto in a dismal room in Paris with black
specks on the wall feeling

The maybe I'm just getting blotto feeling

The trees are no longer my friends feeling

The my friends are no longer my friends feeling

The once I was a nineteenth-century Russian novel but now I'm a frozen
chicken entrée feeling

The I can always return this feeling in the prepaid envelope provided feeling

The I am the prepaid envelope feeling

THE MIRACULOUS

The band starts the song over,
the rhythms still wrong, sounds that will never
alchemize to music. My brother's
new liver is failing. There's someone's loud lover
swearing to Christ and the bar to get sober
but the moon is being smothered
by the trees and there is no ladder
far enough. I go down to the mouth of the river

ugly with waste. Yellow foam and trash. A tanker
crawling the horizon. What does it bear—
oil or chemicals. I was taught a man could walk on water.
That if I listened, and unhinged my heart, I'd hear
a presence stirring the air. And I do: God, the murderer
making things perfectly clear.

ARRIVAL IN ITALY

The train winds north, sounding like an accordion.
Here's where the poet's heart refused to burn.
Here the god killed a white bull who became the moon.
Robed martyrs are floating into everywhere heaven;
sheep are shitting gracefully in the sunflowers,
and Piero della Francesca has solved the equation
for Beauty. She opens her tent, inviting you in.
You're a long way from gleaning dinner
from a freezer bag. Have some drizzled figs.
Cocktails will be served in an hour
in the castle hall, under the skull chandelier.

STILL TIME

in Severn's letters Keats is still alive, though coughing blood,

one day he's better, then things look very bad and if you stop

reading he's still lying there, calmer again and clearer

before they take his body out and burn the wallpaper.

In books you fall in love with, you always slow down

a few pages before the end but then there you are

with only the back-cover blurbs that say

This story will make you cry and maybe an outdated photo.

When you photograph the famous fountain the water

stops moving, but water never really stops moving.

Your plush lion swirled away, your parents floated off, okay but also

that wine stain on your shirt only looked permanent.

After the horrifying bats in the cenote, little gold-flecked fish appeared.

You finally stopped sobbing in the bathroom at weddings.

You can't go back to 1821 and invent streptomycin,

or stop the poet's kindly doctor from bleeding his patient,

but you can climb the stairs to that room in Rome

and see the flowers on the ceiling, the same ones Keats held

for weeks in his fevered gaze. That's as close as you can get.

Go home. Your miserable bitch of a neighbor is gone,

carried out and never to return.

HAPPINESS REPORT

I was happy when I was drunk one night in 1985
squatting in the already pee-wet grass next to Jill Somebody
outside the graduate student poetry reading

And in spite of going off my medication
I was happy today under the hot shower, and again licking cappuccino foam
in front of the air conditioner before I went outside
and sweated through my new shirt like a lying politician in a TV interview

I felt happy while buying the shirt though it wasn't a pure happiness
stained as it was with a price tag
It's hard to find a happy artist because art
requires suffering, goes one theory nearly everyone buys into
getting free subscriptions for their friends

On the wall of the museum, patrons could finish the sentence
Before I die I want to _____.
and someone wrote *be happy*
and another *eat KFC*
but a third wrote *cancel my life* and I bet that person was an artist
or at least more sensitive than the one with a bucket list
that included tortured chickens
I hate the term bucket list

which sounds to me like molded plastic instead of stainless steel and pocked
with little holes your feelings fall through

Some artist said it's better to fall from a great height
but I don't know about that
Maybe great happiness is an abyss
Maybe looking down all you see is a big lake and your own face floating
    there
looking back self-righteously
so it's probably best to crawl under a sympathetic rock

I don't know why the Declaration of Independence talks about the pursuit
    of happiness
when Jefferson originally wrote property
Life, liberty, and property
Maybe I would be happier if I owned some
Some of my ancestors owned slaves
and some were impoverished Italian peasants
Maybe all freedoms are stained

Before I die I'd like to see some changes made
but it's probably too late
just as it's too late to drink myself to death at a young age

That day at the museum I thought *I want to climb to a great height and then*
   fall through myself
the way a man falls through me when I'm happy and in love
Now I only want espresso and a little foam
To stay in bed all day, Christmas lights blinking against the August heat
Pigeons landing outside on the air conditioner walking around making soft
   noises
and then fucking off
Someone screaming in the street who isn't me

I CAN'T STOP LOVING YOU JOHN KEATS

Even though you've been dead for almost two hundred years, I feel like
    maybe
I could fall through a wormhole or get knocked on the head or go through
    some stones in Scotland

& somehow make my way to you, wearing a complicated bonnet of feathers
    & ribbons
with medicines sewn into my pantaloons under my white muslin dress

You'd fall for me & forget about Fanny Brawne & the big difference in our
    ages, because
well, because that's what I want to happen, John Keats, not the part where
    your brother

grows pale & mist-rising-from-a-shorn-field-under-a-sky-of-whirling-
    swallows-thin & yes I'm sorry dies
but the part where we lie on the grass & drink French wine & you lay your
    head on my breast

I can feel your eyelashes against my skin even here in the twenty-first
    century
like the legs of a fly as it lands on a musk-rose while a tiny chorus hymns
    around your head

That's how much I fancy you, John Keats, like you're an Amazon
	fulfillment center far out in space
& I have a Groupon code for an intergalactic shopping spree

like you're the star of a miniseries about a Romantic poet unsullied by
	mycobacteria
& I'm a woman from the future changing literary history forever

writing your name in my diary while you steer our little boat out of Lethe
	& into the lilies
trailing my hand in the canonical water

Please take me away in my tight corset & wedding dress of sand
I don't want to stay in this world watching Truth bound & gagged on the
	railroad tracks

feeling like a fish trapped in a European pedicure spa while the tiny,
	whining violins of privilege play
& Beauty slowly backs away

ART OF POETRY

Between coffee & fentanyl, between Love Me & Go Fuck Yourself
there's so much life to be gotten through
So many mirrors to challenge in your ragged robe & collagen essence
  Korean facial mask

Eventually you have to go out & walk around in the world like you belong
  there
You have to smile at work, & buy things
when you just want to crawl into a closet & live in an old cowboy boot &
  write witty unhinged verses

which sometime before the death of the sun
an advanced civilization will discover, etched into the ancient leather,
  preserved in a rock formation
& display in a luminous floating interdimensional sphere

Q: Ever notice how many writers write about writing?

A few centuries ago Horace wrote approvingly of a poet
He intends not smoke from flame, but light from smoke
which I think is good advice if you can follow it
but he also said that to paint a dolphin in the trees or a boar in the waves

is an unnatural distortion & I thought about how much I'd like to see that

& how unrealistic it is to expect things to stay in their places

Why not someone's grieving widow consoled by a nebula

A suicide vomiting flowers

In the twentieth century Pablo Neruda wrote his own "Arte Poética"

lamenting all the things that called to him without being answered

& reading it, I thought about that time in a tiny fishing village in Mexico,

a third mangorita waterfalling through my liver

the waitress coming toward me in a white T-shirt with black lettering that

    said

I HAVE NO TITS

which was clearly a lie although her stomach was kind of big which had the

    effect

of making them appear to recede

like the single taillights of two antique Model A Fords sputtering together

    toward obsolescence

Q: Does she even know what it says?

I HAVE NO TITS

What is the message, is this perhaps a code, could it be from the future

Is it a "Ceci n'est pas une pipe" situation like in that painting of a pipe

or a new far-reaching campaign from the U.S. Ministry of Enlightenment

    & Propaganda

The thieving president wearing a golfing shirt that says I HAVE NO

    CLOTHES

Q: Who killed poetry again & who cares?

Between false flags & homeless laundry lines

Between long-lasting eyebrow gel & little-known destinations profiled in

    the *New York Times*

I don't know where anyone is going or where there is to get to

The days & nights keep drunkenly arriving, the guests are all dying

& I'm starting to feel pretty sick

BABIES AT PARADISE POND

from a lithograph by Sandy Skoglund

I don't know what to make of these scary babies
Pale babies naked on their backs flailing in the grass
crawling & staggering baldly around

like abortions swarming in a dream, full-grown & seed-eyed
like newly molting cockroach nymphs flushed out of hiding

like a medieval brochure for Baby Limbo
on the Banks of Pristine Paradise Pond:
As Close as They Can Get to the Beatific Vision!

They look like dolls dropped from outer space
by a giant petulant girl creature with twenty-six arms
throwing up her twenty-six hands all at once, then running out of the galaxy
& slamming it behind her

A picture of so many babies should be happy & maybe it is for some people
if they don't look too closely
which is the only way I know how to truly be happy
Things look so much better in the subaqueous glow of the bar on a third
   glass of wine
I love the world most when I can barely make out what's going on out there

The little dog down at the edge of the pond might be licking that baby
or eating it

Even the grownups are scary, gazing out over the water
toward the dispirited trees & the invisible source of the light

Creepy pre-birth or post-death light
Spaceship tractor beam of the many-armed mother
picking up all the toys

Oh as usual all I can see is time & death
Everything is already lost
& not coming back

LITTLE OLD LADIES

We know we're supposed to shut up now & tremble off
into the wilderness of a golf course on the edge of a retirement community
& fall down crying in a sand trap
moaning about the sadistic hurricane of time
that's flattened our downtown & ruined our hayfields and barns

We're supposed to stand out in the rain-starved pasture like cows about to
        get tipped
& no good for milking
Some kids are vaping in their truck at the edge of the field, getting up their
        courage
Those pink clouds have moved off to the east & night is wrapping the world
in a crappy torn sweater

The pharma companies are drawing near, promising many indelicate side
        effects
in a soothing voiceover
Young professionals lining us up on city view balconies to be shoved off
Internet scammers lasering targets on our foreheads

Light flashes in our eyes
the vitreous gel detaching from the retina
our skin loosening & separating from our weak little bones

It's just like a fairy tale, we're turning into birds—ortolans
about to be dined on in dark institutions

Soon we'll be pissing vodka in our bedpans
pulling the fire alarm, wandering out into traffic
No one will know about our epic journeys down the hall
sailing to the dining room & back
or the monsters we had to bitch slap to come this far & survive

So we're telling you now in our little old voices
while we wait to be scraped away
like worn paint, while you turn from us to the window & open the plastic
    curtains
not wanting to breathe us in

DEATH & MEMORY

Some people are remembered for being beheaded . . .
& some for autoerotic asphyxiation . . .

Some people open the cage door & step in with the tiger
deliberately or accidentally . . .
Either may boost their book sales briefly . . . which is seldom the reason . . .
It's more like a pleasant but unintended outcome . . . that they can't enjoy . . .

Occasionally people are remembered for being lethally injected . . . but
     more often
pets are kept in mind . . . their ashes in a box labeled with a photograph . . .
Photographs are useful for remembering the dead . . . but not that useful . . .

Dreams of the dead are better because you don't know you're dreaming . . .
But when you wake up you know . . .
& waking life is full of death every minute . . .

Some people are remembered with exhausting biographies
& maybe a quasi-historical mini-series . . . featuring people with better teeth
& many plot-serving inaccuracies . . .

Others just fall into tiny crevasses & disappear
like a river of termites . . .

It's hard to keep thinking of the dead . . . when they never call or text . . .
like people you used to be in love with . . . who said they couldn't live
  without you . . .

Patron saints are dead people . . . & some people talk to them . . .
but saints are strangers . . . who lived a long time ago, in itchy clothes . . .
& religion is a waste of time . . . when you could be drinking . . .

Some people talk to their ancestors & say they talk back . . .
but my ancestors just lie there . . . like badly stored cigars . . .

Not even my parents will speak to me . . .
They just linger underground
in a smaller & smaller font . . .

No one knows what happens when you die . . .
except for the gases & putrefaction . . .
Death is a story with a terrible beginning . . . & dead people
are passive characters . . .

Maybe it's better to forget them . . . so they don't trouble you . . .
like trauma . . . or commercial jingles . . .
so you can continue . . . living . . .

STAY

So your device has a low battery & seems to drain faster each day.
Maybe you should double your medication.

You might feel queasy, but also as if the spatula flattening you to the fry pan
has lifted a little.

So your breath comes out scorched, so what.

Inside, trust me on this,
there's a ribbon of beach by a lake,

in the sand, fragments of a fossilized creature resembling a tulip.

Back in the Paleozoic, online wasn't invented yet
so everyone had to wander alone & miserable through the volcanic wastes

or just glue themselves to a rock hoping someone would pass by.

Now you can sob to an image of your friend a continent away
& be consoled.

Please wait for the transmissions, however faint.

Listen: when a stranger steps into the elevator with a bouquet of white
   roses not meant for you,

they're meant for you.

ACKNOWLEDGMENTS

Gratitude to the editors of the following journals for previous publication of these poems:

Adroit Journal (www.theadroitjournal.org): "Ghosted"

American Journal of Poetry: "Babies at Paradise Pond"

American Poetry Review: "Animals," "Archive of Recent Uncomfortable Emotions"

Five Points: "Art of Poetry," "Ex"

James Dickey Review: "August," "Comfort of the Resurrection"

Literary Matters (www.literarymatters.org): "High Desert, New Mexico"

Los Angeles Review of Books: "AlienMatch.com" (as "aliens.com"),"Wolf Song"

The New Yorker: "Ways of Being Lonely"

Plume Poetry 8: "Song for Sad Girls"

Plume Poetry 9: "Small Talk"

Plume (www.plumepoetry.com): "Résumé"

Shrew: "I Can't Stop Loving You John Keats"

Southword (Ireland): "Black Hour Blues," "Happiness Report," "The Miraculous," "Still Time"

Washington Square Review: "Stay," "The Truth"

Women's Review of Books: "All Hallows," "Little Old Ladies," "Telepathy"

"Babies at Paradise Pond" also appeared in *The Ekphrastic Writer*, edited by Janée J. Baugher.

"Black Hour Blues" was awarded Third Prize in the Gregory O'Donoghue Poetry Competition (Ireland), 2017.

"Grace," "To the Woman Crying Uncontrollably in the Next Stall," and "Winter Solstice" appeared in *The Night Could Go in Either Direction*, a collaborative chapbook with Brittany Perham, from Slapering Hol Press in 2016. "To The Woman Crying Uncontrollably in the Next Stall" also appeared in the anthologies *Nasty Women Poets*, edited by Grace Bauer and Julie Kane, and *Women of Resistance: Poems for a New Feminism*, edited by Danielle Barnhart and Iris Mahan; and online at *Diode* and the *Paris Review* blog, *Poetry RX*.

"Guitar" previously appeared in *Across the Waves: Contemporary Poetry from Ireland and the United States*, edited by Gerry LaFemina.

"High Desert, New Mexico" was also featured on BBC Radio 4's "The Lightning Field," September 8, 2018.

"People You Don't Know" received First Prize in the 2018 Mick Imlah Poetry Prize competition and appeared in the *Times Literary Supplement* (UK).

"The Earth Is About Used Up" takes its title from a line by Paul Guest.

Thanks to the Civitella Ranieri Foundation, the Camargo Foundation, and La Romita School of Art, where some of these poems were conceived. Thanks to Susan Browne, Sara Jane Hall, Emily Lindner, Donna Masini, Brittany Perham, and Elizabeth Sanderson, inspirations all.

ABOUT THE AUTHOR

Kim Addonizio is the author of several previous poetry collections including *Tell Me*, a finalist for the National Book Award. Her other books include a memoir, *Bukowski in a Sundress: Confessions from a Writing Life*, two novels, two story collections, and two books on writing poetry: *The Poet's Companion: A Guide to the Pleasures of Writing Poetry* (with Dorianne Laux) and *Ordinary Genius: A Guide for the Poet Within*. She has received numerous honors for her work, including two NEA Fellowships, a Guggenheim Fellowship, and Pushcart Prizes in both poetry and the essay. Her poetry has been translated into several languages including Arabic, Chinese, Spanish, and Italian. She is an occasional presenter for BBC Radio and teaches privately in Oakland, California, and online. www.kimaddonizio.com.